D0471046

UNDERSTANDING THE HUMAN BODY

Heart, Blood, and Lungs

by

Steve Parker

Please visit our web site at: www.garethstevens.com
For a free color catalog describing Gareth Stevens Publishing's list of high-quality books and multimedia programs, call 1-800-542-2595 (USA) or 1-800-387-3178 (Canada). Gareth Stevens Publishing's fax: (414) 332-3567.

Library of Congress Cataloging-in-Publication Data

Parker, Steve.
    Heart, blood, and lungs / by Steve Parker.
        p. cm. — (Understanding the human body)
    Includes index.
    ISBN 0-8368-4206-5 (lib. bdg.)
    1. Cardiopulmonary system—Juvenile literature. I. Title. II. Series.
QP103.P373   2004
612.1—dc22   2004045328

This North American edition first published in 2005 by
Gareth Stevens Publishing
A World Almanac Education Group Company
330 West Olive Street, Suite 100
Milwaukee, WI 53212 USA

This U.S. edition copyright © 2005 by Gareth Stevens, Inc. Original edition copyright © 2004 ticktock Entertainment Ltd. First published in Great Britain in 2004 by ticktock Media Ltd., Unit 2, Orchard Business Centre, North Farm Road, Tunbridge Wells, Kent, TN2 3XF.

We would like to thank Elizabeth Wiggans, Jenni Rainford, and Dr. Kristina Routh for their help with this book.

Consultant: Dr. Kristina Routh
Gareth Stevens editor: Carol Ryback
Gareth Stevens designer: Scott M. Krall

Picture credits: t (top), b (bottom), c (center), l (left), r (right)
Alamy: Cover (left), 5tl, 9tc, 9c, 9bc, 12tl, 13c, 14-15c, 15c, 18tl, 19tc, 19cr, 20bc, 21tc, 22-23c, 24bc, 25c, 25tr, 25cr, 26bc, 27tl, 28b. Mediscan:12-13c, 13t. Primal Pictures: Cover (right), 7tr, 9tr, 11tr, 13tr, 15tr, 17tr, 19tr, 20-21c, 21tr, 21cr, 23tr, 27tr, 29tr, 29cr. Science Photo Library: 4 (all), 9br, 11c, 13cr, 15bc, 17tc, 19c, 23cr, 26tl, 27tc, 27b, 29-30c, 29br, 30tl.

Every effort has been made to trace the copyright holders, and we apologize in advance for any unintentional omissions. We would be pleased to insert the appropriate acknowledgments in any subsequent edition of this publication.

Printed in the United States of America

1 2 3 4 5 6 7 8 9 08 07 06 05 04

GARETH**STEVENS**
GS
PUBLISHING
A World Almanac Education Group Company

How to use this book

This book is your guide to yourself—an atlas of the human body. Follow the main text for an informative overview of a particular area of the body or use the boxes to jump to a specific area of interest. Finally, try some of the suggested activities and experiments to discover more about yourself!

Body Locator

Highlighted areas on the body locator help you learn your body's geography by indicating the area of the body organs or systems discussed on those pages.

Instant Info

Get instant, snappy facts that summarize the topic in just a few sentences. Learn how often the heart beats every minute, how much air the lungs can hold, how the blood carries oxygen, and much more.

Health Watch

Read about illness and disease related to the relevant area of the body. For example, learn what happens to our arteries if we eat too many fatty foods.

INSTANT FACT

If the body was as big as a large city like London or New York, **its main blood vessels would be like motorways 150 metres across,** and its tiniest vessels would be about the width of a pencil.

The heart, blood and all the blood vessels make up about **one tenth of the weight of the whole body.**

If all the blood vessels in the body could be joined end to end, **they would go around the world more than twice.**

HEALTHWATCH

What we eat, drink and do every day all have huge effects on our heart and blood vessels. Smoking, too much food rich in animals fats, lack of exercise and being overweight cause big problems. They are known as 'risk factors' for heart disease. Each risk factor on its own has a bad effect, and two or more combined make the risk to our health much worse.

Heart *Engine of Life*

We each have one bag-shaped muscle that never rests or relaxes—our hearts. A multichambered pump for the circulatory system, your heart automatically adjusts its rate to your needs. Every heartbeat forces blood through the network of blood vessels around your body.

Around and Around
Our blood circulates (goes around and around) in a closed system as it delivers oxygen to all body parts, organs, and tissues. Blood also carries hundreds of other substances. These include energy-packed sugars, nutrients for growth, vitamins and minerals to keep the body working well, disease-fighting white blood cells, and "messenger" substances, or hormones, that control many bodily processes.

Always Busy
Blood not only delivers—it also collects. On its journey through the body, blood gathers up wastes formed by cells and tissues. Your lungs rid the blood of waste gases, such as carbon dioxide. Your two kidneys filter (remove) unwanted substances carried by the blood and form the waste liquid, urine. Blood also helps us keep our bodies at a steady temperature. As it circulates around the body, blood spreads heat from hard-working parts like the heart and muscles to cooler areas like the limbs and skin. If the body gets too hot, blood vessels in the skin widen to help the body lose that extra warmth to the surrounding air.

Any movement makes muscles work harder and requires extra supplies of oxygen and energy. The heart pumps harder and faster to increase blood flow to the muscles.

Diagrams

Watch for in-depth scientific diagrams and explanations that focus on the details of a body part.

Metric Conversion Table on page 31

In Focus

View stunning macroimagery
and other images of an anatomically
correct digital model of body parts.

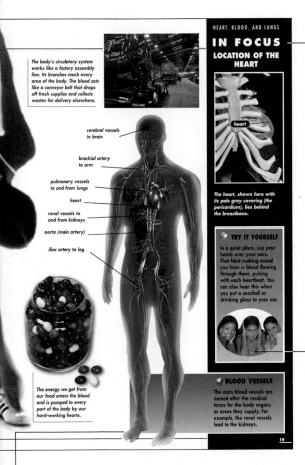

The body's circulatory system works like a factory assembly line. Its branches reach every area of the body. The blood acts like a conveyor belt that drops off fresh supplies and collects wastes for delivery elsewhere.

cerebral vessels in brain

brachial artery to arm

pulmonary vessels to and from lungs

heart

renal vessels to and from kidneys

aorta (main artery)

iliac artery to leg

The energy we get from our food enters the blood and is pumped to every part of the body by our hard-working hearts.

HEART, BLOOD, AND LUNGS

IN FOCUS
LOCATION OF THE HEART

heart

The heart, shown here with its pale gray covering (the pericardium), lies behind the breastbone.

TRY IT YOURSELF

In a quiet place, cup your hands over your ears. That faint rushing sound you hear is blood flowing through them, pulsing with each heartbeat. You can also hear this when you put a seashell or drinking glass to your ear.

BLOOD VESSELS

The main blood vessels are named after the medical terms for the body organs or areas they supply. For example, the renal vessels lead to the kidneys.

19

Try It Yourself

Try these suggested activities to
learn more. No special equipment
is required—just your own body!

CONTENTS

Introduction

Space-walking astronauts, firefighters in smoke-filled buildings, and scuba divers have one thing in common—they carry an air supply with them. The human body cannot last for long without taking in oxygen, one of the gases found in the air we breathe. But getting fresh air into the lungs is only half the story. Once the oxygen is inside, it must travel to every tiny nook and cranny of the body. This is the job of the heart and blood.

Never Breathless

Body parts that work together for one major purpose are known as a body system. The respiratory system—the air passages through the nose and throat, the trachea (windpipe), lungs, and chest muscles—functions as a unit to deliver essential oxygen to the body. Our bodies demand a constant supply of this vital gas, so we breathe every few seconds of every minute, every day—and all night, too.

Never Beatless

The circulatory system consists of a central pump (the heart), the blood vessels that branch from it, and the blood flowing through those vessels. Like breathing, our heartbeats never stop, day and night, year after year. Our beating hearts deliver blood, its all-important oxygen, and a host of other substances necessary for life and health to all parts of our bodies.

When we are active, our bodies need more oxygen. We breathe faster and harder, and our heart rates increase to pump blood around our bodies more quickly.

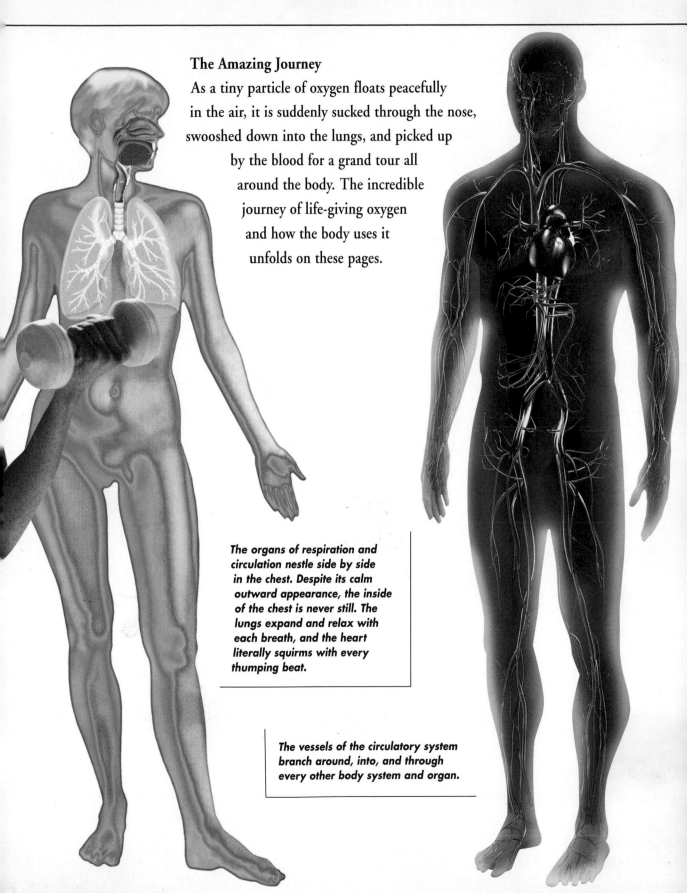

The Amazing Journey

As a tiny particle of oxygen floats peacefully in the air, it is suddenly sucked through the nose, swooshed down into the lungs, and picked up by the blood for a grand tour all around the body. The incredible journey of life-giving oxygen and how the body uses it unfolds on these pages.

The organs of respiration and circulation nestle side by side in the chest. Despite its calm outward appearance, the inside of the chest is never still. The lungs expand and relax with each breath, and the heart literally squirms with every thumping beat.

The vessels of the circulatory system branch around, into, and through every other body system and organ.

The respiratory system of an adult holds between 4 quarts and 6 quarts of air.

The nose, throat, and trachea (windpipe) hold almost half a pint of air.

About 1 quart of air always stays in the lungs, no matter how hard we breathe out.

Each year, an adult breathes enough air to fill about half of the Goodyear blimp. Over a lifetime, a person takes about half a billion breaths.

The respiratory system's self-cleaning passageways rid the body of normal amounts of dust, smoke, floating powder, chemicals, and dirt, but large amounts or repeated exposure to them can cause great damage. Use a mask or respirator to trap such particles before you breathe them into your respiratory system. Cigarette smoke is one of the most common lung irritants around.

Lungs *Many Airways*

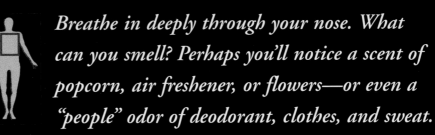

Breathe in deeply through your nose. What can you smell? Perhaps you'll notice a scent of popcorn, air freshener, or flowers—or even a "people" odor of deodorant, clothes, and sweat.

As you breathe in, oxygen begins a journey through your respiratory system that could end at your fingers or toes!

Oxygen Needs

The respiratory system's main purpose is to bring oxygen into the body. Oxygen helps the body process food to release the energy it contains. This process, called cellular respiration, occurs many times every second in every cell of the body. The energy released by cellular respiration powers hundreds of other life processes performed by cells. The term can be confusing because the action of breathing is also called respiration.

We can breathe in through our noses or mouths. The nose specializes in taking in air, while the mouth is usually considered part of the digestive system.

Poisonous Waste

Our cells need a continuous supply of oxygen. As the cells use oxygen, they produce a waste gas called carbon dioxide. This gas becomes poisonous if too much builds up inside the body. Carbon dioxide leaves our bodies when we breathe out. Our respiratory systems also help with our sense of smell and the power of speech.

The inner linings of the airways and lungs are moist. We breathe this dampness out as water vapor. If the air around us is cold, the vapor condenses, or turns back into tiny droplets of water—"cold steam."

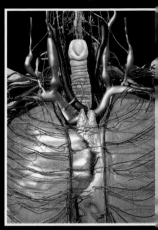

A front view reveals the vocal folds at the top of the trachea and shows how high in the chest the lungs extend.

Most kinds of medical scans, like this chest X ray, show solid body parts such as bones in white. Air-filled breathing passages and lungs appear as dark areas.

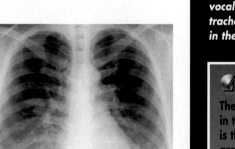

AIRWAYS

The main passage for air in the respiratory system is through the nose, around the rear of the palate to the throat, and down the trachea to the lungs in the chest.

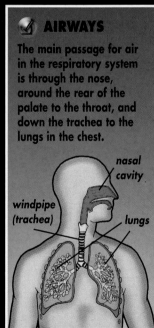

nasal cavity

windpipe (trachea)

lungs

Inhalation (breathing in) is an automatic process. We usually don't think about it or try to regulate it unless we are exercising hard or notice an enjoyable scent or perfume. Likewise, exhalation, or breathing out, is usually automatic. Blowing at a feather is a type of specialized exhalation.

TRY IT YOURSELF

How many ways can you breathe out? We often use out-breaths to show our thoughts and emotions without speaking. You could breathe out softly as a sigh of sadness, or slightly harder when you give up on a problem, or harder still to show irritation.

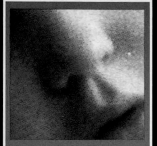

Every day, the inside lining of your nose makes about enough mucus to fill up a normal-sized egg.

Air normally flows in and out of the nose at a speed of almost 7 feet per second, or about 5 miles per hour.

When we cough, air rushes out through the mouth at 66 feet per second, or 45 miles per hour (mph).

Sneezing blasts air out of the nose at 95 feet per second (65 mph).

HEALTH WATCH

Some people have an allergy or sensitivity to tiny floating particles in air, such as dust or plant pollen. The lining inside the nose reacts to "fight" these particles as if they were harmful germs. The lining becomes swollen and itchy, which causes a runny nose and sneezing. The general name for this condition is allergic rhinitis. Allergy to pollen is sometimes called "hay fever."

Lungs *Upper Airways*

Sniff, sniff, blow . . . when you have a cold, spend time outside in windy winter weather, or shed a few tears, your nose may drip or run. You can clear it by blowing into a facial tissue or handkerchief. A runny nose is very annoying, but the slimy, sticky mucus has a vital job. Mucus keeps the delicate lining moist and helps the nose catch germs.

Inside the Nose

The nose is the body's air-conditioning unit. It warms, moistens, and filters incoming air. The nose's two holes, or nostrils, lead into twin air spaces called nasal chambers. Each is bigger than a thumb, lined with damp mucus, and rich in tiny blood vessels. Your nose plays an important role in preparing the air for entry into the very delicate lung tissues.

Smoke, powder, and dust are visible forms of air pollution, but many harmful gases, vapors, and fumes are invisible. They include the tiny particles emitted by vehicles, especially those powered by diesel engines.

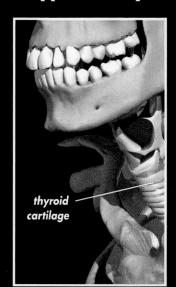

thyroid cartilage

The large, curved thyroid cartilage in the front of the upper neck, with two prongs facing up and down at each side, protects the lower throat, vocal folds, and trachea.

Down the Throat

Hairs in the nostrils trap dirt and dust, while the mucus-covered lining inside the nasal chambers captures tiny particles such as germs. The nose also filters and cleans the air—unlike air breathed in through the mouth, which goes directly to the lungs. The nasal mucus is constantly being made and falling off. It usually passes into the throat and is swallowed. We remove excess mucus caused by infection or irritation by blowing our noses.

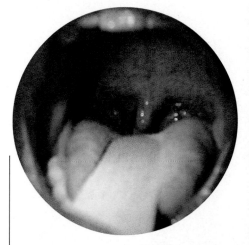

Tonsils are the lumpy patches at the back of the pharynx (throat). Part of the disease-fighting immune system, tonsils may become swollen, red, and painful when infected with germs.

✓ SINUSES

Small passageways that branch out from the nasal chambers lead to the sinuses—four pairs of spongelike, air-filled spaces inside the facial skull bones.

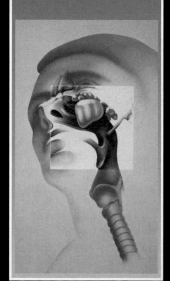

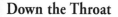

Ahhh-chooooo! A sneeze blasts air up the throat, through the nasal chambers, and out the nose and mouth. Sneezing clears blocked or itchy nasal passages. Bright lights, pollen, or smoke often cause sneezing.

🖐 TRY IT YOURSELF

Speak normally. Now hold your nose and talk. Your voice sounds very different. During normal speech, sounds come out through the mouth and nose. The nasal chambers and sinuses give the voice a fuller, richer sound. Holding your nose while talking prevents this.

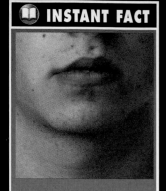
Lungs *Vocal Folds and Speech*

If you ever tried to get a message to someone through a window or in a loud crowd, you probably realized the importance of your voice. We can send written messages a number of ways, but the sounds we make using the voicebox (larynx) are our main way of communicating with others.

In the Neck

The voicebox, or larynx, lies between the base of the throat and the upper part of the trachea. Its main structure is made of curved parts of cartilage, which is similar to bone but slightly softer and more flexible. The largest, called the thyroid cartilage, forms a bulge commonly known as the "Adam's apple" under the skin in the front of the neck.

Folds, Not Cords

The larynx contains two vocal "cords" that are actually folds or ridges, one on either side, that stick out into the airway. Normally, the vocal folds are separated so we can breathe without making a sound through

IN FOCUS
Down to the Chest

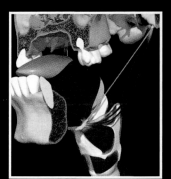

The leaf-shaped flap of epiglottis cartilage sits above your larynx. When you swallow food, this flap folds down over the larynx to prevent any food from entering the airway and causing choking.

To speak or sing higher notes, the muscles in the voicebox pull the vocal folds and stretch them tighter so they vibrate

the gap between them, (known as the glottis). To make sounds, muscles pull the vocal folds almost together, leaving just a narrow gap. As air passes up from the lungs and through this gap, it makes the vocal folds vibrate. These vibrations make the basic sounds of the voice. Our throats, mouths, nose chambers, and sinuses make these noises louder, and the tongue, teeth, and lips help us produce clear speech.

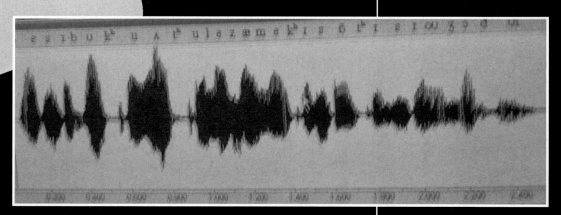

No two people have exactly the same shape of larynx, throat, nose, and mouth, so each person's voice is unique. A picture of the voice's sound waves is called a sonogram, or "voiceprint." A person's voiceprint is as individual as his or her fingerprints and can be used for identification or security purposes.

 TRY IT YOURSELF

Feel your voicebox while humming. You should detect the vibrations. Make the hum louder, and the vibrations become stronger. Change your lip positions to make "eeee" and "oooo" sounds, and see how the mouth alters the basic sound of the vocal folds. Now make a hissing sound like a snake, and the voicebox vibrations stop. The hiss is from air passing through a narrow gap between the tongue and roof of the mouth.

VOICEBOX

The voicebox (larynx) is a chamber of complicated shape made of cartilage, muscles, and ligaments. The vocal folds in the larynx are ridges that vibrate to make sounds.

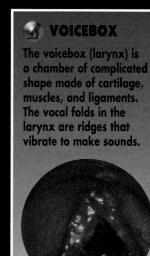

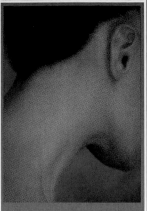
An adult's trachea is about 4 inches long and 1 inch wide.

Sixteen to twenty C-shaped pieces of cartilage strengthen the trachea's walls.

The right main bronchus is 1 inch long, and the left one is usually about twice as long.

If all the different-sized air tubes in the lungs could be joined end to end, they would stretch more than 31 miles.

👁 HEALTH WATCH

Asthma is an allergic condition that causes difficult and wheezy breathing. Dust, chemicals, or plant pollens floating in the air can bring on an allergic reaction, or asthma attack. Muscles in the airway walls tighten, and the linings of the airway and lungs produce more mucus, which clogs the system.

Lungs *Lower Airways*

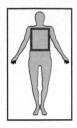

Every time you move your head and neck, you twist and bend your windpipe, or trachea. This is the main airway tube leading down to your chest.

Holding the Airways Open

In order to keep the trachea open against the body's internal pressure, its outer walls are strengthened with C-shaped pieces of cartilage. These make the trachea very strong but flexible enough to stay open and allow a free flow of air, even when internal body organs may push against it. At its lower end, the trachea divides into two slightly smaller tubes (also with cartilage rings), known as bronchi. One bronchus leads to each lung. Each bronchus then divides into smaller tubes, which also divide, and so on.

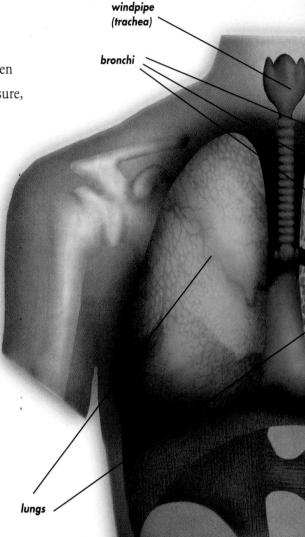

windpipe (trachea)

bronchi

lungs

🌟 TRY IT YOURSELF

Look in a mirror, and then turn your body to face left or right while your head stays looking at the mirror. Notice how your neck twists, yet you can still breathe easily. Then give a small cough to "clear your throat." You are really clearing your lungs by coughing old mucus with bits of dust and germs up toward your trachea and mouth. Then you can spit it out.

During a bronchoscopy, doctors use a bronchoscope—a lighted tube with a camera—to look down the throat into the trachea and bronchi. This procedure reveals tumors, blockages, infection, and other problems.

The branching pattern of air tubes in the lungs is known as the bronchial tree. Its narrowest "twigs" (not shown here) extend into every part of each lung. The bronchial tree sways as the lungs inflate and deflate, bending like a live, outside tree with each breath.

Keeping Clean

Like the inside of the nose, the "self-cleaning" lining of the trachea, bronchi, and bronchioles continuously produces a thin layer of sticky mucus to trap dust and germs. Millions of tiny hairs, called cilia, cover the lining and beat to push the mucus along, back up through the bronchial tubes and trachea, to the throat, where it is regularly swallowed. This cleaning process prevents the lungs from clogging with dirt and germs.

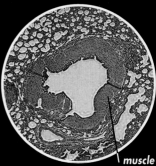

muscle

All but the tiniest airways have a layer of smooth, or involuntary, muscle. Exposure to toxic fumes or allergens makes these muscles constrict (narrow) the airways automatically. The same thing happens during an asthma attack.

Tiny dust mites thrive in dust, carpets, beds, curtains, and furniture. The droppings they leave behind dry into a powder that floats easily and, when breathed in, can cause the wheeziness of asthma.

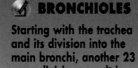

The trachea splits into two large tubes that divide again and again into smaller airways that bring air deep into the lungs.

🔎 BRONCHIOLES

Starting with the trachea and its division into the main bronchi, another 23 or so divisions result in thousands of tiny air tubes, called bronchioles, that reach into the lungs. When someone suffers an asthma attack, these tiny airways contract and cause breathing difficulties.

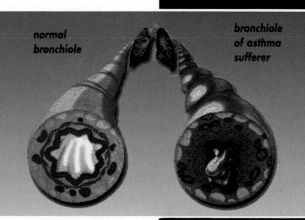

normal bronchiole

bronchiole of asthma sufferer

Each lung contains about 300 million tiny air sacs called alveoli.

As you breathe, those millions of alveoli inflate and deflate like miniature balloons. Your lungs hold about three times as much air when you inhale as when you exhale.

The surface area of the capillary blood vessels in the lungs would cover the floor of a 10 x 10 foot room.

HEALTH WATCH

Smoking damages your lungs and can cause an incurable disease called emphysema. Smoke deep inside your lungs can break down delicate lung tissue, increasing the size of the air spaces in your lungs. (Think of tiny soap bubbles breaking up to form a larger bubble.) To imagine what it is like to have emphysema, take a deep breath. Now let out just a little of that air and inhale again. Imagine doing that for the rest of your life.

Lungs *Deep in the Lungs*

Your lung tissue is wrapped and packed so efficiently into your chest that if spread out, it would cover one side of a singles tennis court. This huge surface area of your respiratory, or pulmonary, organs allows you to inhale plenty of oxygen.

Tiny Bubbles

By the time the airways in your lungs have branched more than 20 times, they are thinner than hairs and number more than 10 million. Each of these tiny tubules is called a terminal bronchiole. At the end of each terminal bronchiole lies a bunch of bubble-shaped air spaces, called alveoli, that look like grapes on a stalk. These alveoli make up about one-half of the total volume of the lung tissue. The rest of the lung tissue consists of the various branching airways

the branching pulmonary arteries that bring oxygen-

they become smaller and smaller until they form capillaries, the body's tiniest blood vessels.

Capillaries surround each alveolus like a net. The walls of the capillaries are only one cell thick, so that waste gases in the blood pass easily to the air inside each alveolus and are removed as you breathe out. As you breathe in, you pull oxygen from the air into your many alveoli, where it seeps through the capillaries to your blood. From there, the oxygen-rich blood travels to the heart, which pumps it throughout the rest of your body.

IN FOCUS
Chest Contents

airways

This illustration of the chest with the heart and lungs removed shows the branching airways and blood vessels within the breathing muscles of the rib cage.

If the inside of your chest was one large, hollow space, it would have a surface area of slightly more than a square yard or meter. But because your airways divide so many times, the surface area for gas exchange is more than 100 times about the size of a tennis court.

lung cancer

This chest X-ray reveals lung cancer, most likely caused by smoking.

🐚 ALVEOLI

A microscopic look at lung tissue reveals alveoli and capillary blood vessels. This is where the blood exchanges its carbon dioxide for oxygen and becomes bright red.

✋ TRY IT YOURSELF

To get an idea of how much air your lungs can hold, take a very deep breath and blow up a balloon. Keep blowing until your breath runs out and your lungs feel empty. Notice how the balloon changes in size. Now squeeze all the air out of it. Unlike a balloon, you can never breathe out all the air from deep inside your lungs.

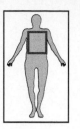

HEALTH WATCH

The respiratory system provides a route for germs to enter the body. Nose hairs and mucus help filter and trap germs, but some still pass through the delicate linings inside the nose, throat, or lungs. They cause various infections, such as colds or sore throats. A sneeze can spray germ-laden droplets up to 10 feet. Cover your nose and mouth with a tissue to avoid spreading germs when you cough or sneeze.

Lungs *Breathing*

Breathing is one of our most basic, automatic functions—but one that we can also control. We regulate our breathing when we talk, eat, drink, or blow our noses.

In with the Fresh Air

Like other body movements, muscles power breathing. Normal breathing involves two sets of muscles. The diaphragm, a curved sheet of muscles shaped like an upside-down bowl, separates the lungs from the abdomen. As the diaphram contracts (tightens), it flattens and stretches the bases of the lungs. This pulls air down through the trachea into the lungs. The intercostal muscles between the ribs contract to lift and swing the ribs out as you breathe in. This also stretches the lungs and pulls air into them.

Out with the Stale Air

You use muscles to breathe in but not to breathe out. When you breathe out, the diaphragm and intercostal muscles relax, springing back to their smaller size.

Lungfish can "breathe" three different ways. Like other fish, they breathe oxygen from the water using frilly gills under flaplike covers in the neck region. Lungfish can also gulp air into a baglike organ that works like a lung. Finally, they absorb oxygen through their moist skin.

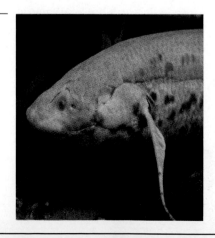

Working muscles cause faster and deeper breathing so that the lungs can bring more oxygen to the blood. Make deep breathing easier by stooping slightly—with arms forward and down—until you catch your breath.

A peak flow meter measures the force and amount of air blown out of the lungs. After a patient blows hard into the tube-shaped device, doctors use the measurement to identify or monitor respiratory problems such as asthma.

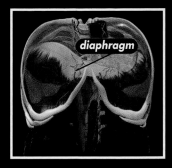

The double-domed, sheet-shaped diaphragm muscle forms the boundary between the thorax (chest) and the abdomen. The body's major blood vessels and the esophagus pass through the diaphragm.

This blows out the stale air that contains more carbon dioxide than oxygen from the lungs. Two slippery, baglike cover layers, called pleurae, surround the lungs and allow them to slide easily against the inside of the chest as they inflate and deflate with each breath.

TRY IT YOURSELF

Sit quietly for five minutes. Next count the number of breaths you take in one minute. ("In" and "out" is one breath.) Now jog or skip for two minutes. Sit down and count your breathing rate each minute for the next three minutes. How fast does your breathing rate return to normal? Compare your results with your friends.

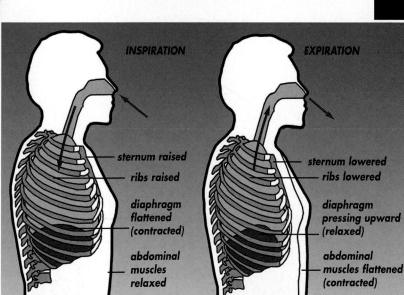

INSPIRATION

- sternum raised
- ribs raised
- diaphragm flattened (contracted)
- abdominal muscles relaxed

EXPIRATION

- sternum lowered
- ribs lowered
- diaphragm pressing upward (relaxed)
- abdominal muscles flattened (contracted)

FLEXIBLE LUNGS

Your lungs change in size with each breath in and out. As you inhale, rib muscles lift your chest up and out, while the diaphragm pushes down on your lower internal organs and makes your belly bulge slightly. These movements give your lungs more room to expand as air flows into them.

If the body was as big as a large city like London or New York, **its main blood vessels would be like motorways 150 metres across**, and its tiniest vessels would be about the width of a pencil.

The heart, blood and all the blood vessels make up about **one tenth of the weight of the whole body.**

If all the blood vessels in the body could be joined end to end, **they would go around the world more than twice.**

👁 HEALTHWATCH

What we eat, drink and do every day all have huge effects on our heart and blood vessels. Smoking, too much food rich in animals fats, lack of exercise and being overweight cause big problems. They are known as 'risk factors' for heart disease. Each risk factor on its own has a bad effect, and two or more combined make the risk to our health much worse.

Heart *Engine of Life*

We each have one bag-shaped muscle that never rests or relaxes—our hearts. A multichambered pump for the circulatory system, your heart automatically adjusts its rate to your needs. Every heartbeat forces blood through the network of blood vessels around your body.

Around and Around

Our blood circulates (goes around and around) in a closed system as it delivers oxygen to all body parts, organs, and tissues. Blood also carries hundreds of other substances. These include energy-packed sugars, nutrients for growth, vitamins and minerals to keep the body working well, disease-fighting white blood cells, and "messenger" substances, or hormones, that control many bodily processes.

Always Busy

Blood not only delivers—it also collects. On its journey through the body, blood gathers up wastes formed by cells and tissues. Your lungs rid the blood of waste gases, such as carbon dioxide. Your two kidneys filter (remove) unwanted substances carried by the blood and form the waste liquid, urine. Blood also helps us keep our bodies at a steady temperature. As it circulates around the body, blood spreads heat from hard-working parts like the heart and muscles to cooler areas like the limbs and skin. If the body gets too hot, blood vessels in the skin widen to help the body lose that extra warmth to the surrounding air.

Any movement makes muscles work harder and requires extra supplies of oxygen and energy. The heart pumps harder and faster to increase blood flow to the muscles.

The body's circulatory system works like a factory assembly line. Its branches reach every area of the body. The blood acts like a conveyor belt that drops off fresh supplies and collects wastes for delivery elsewhere.

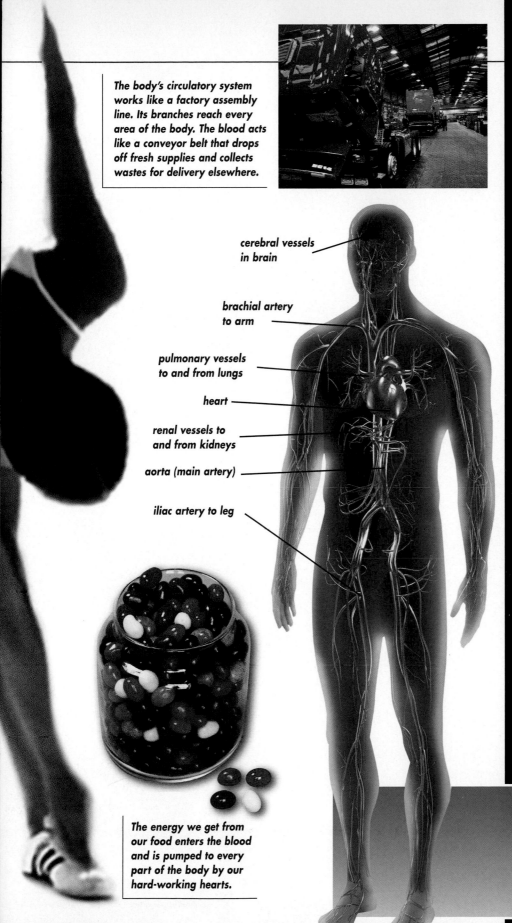

cerebral vessels in brain

brachial artery to arm

pulmonary vessels to and from lungs

heart

renal vessels to and from kidneys

aorta (main artery)

iliac artery to leg

The energy we get from our food enters the blood and is pumped to every part of the body by our hard-working hearts.

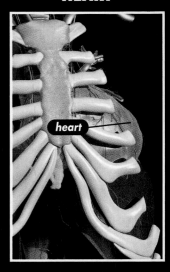

heart

The heart, shown here with its pale gray covering (the pericardium), lies behind the breastbone.

TRY IT YOURSELF

In a quiet place, cup your hands over your ears. That faint rushing sound you hear is blood flowing through them, pulsing with each heartbeat. You can also hear this when you put a seashell or drinking glass to your ear.

BLOOD VESSELS

The main blood vessels are named after the medical terms for the body organs or areas they supply. For example, the renal vessels lead to the kidneys.

The heart is about the size as its owner's clenched fist.

The average weight for an adult man's heart is about 11 ounces—about the same as a medium grapefruit.

The average weight for an adult woman's heart is about 9 ounces.

The lowermost pointed tip of the heart is about level with the sixth rib.

⊙ HEALTH WATCH

Good health habits for the heart begin when you are young. Heart disease, including the clogging of one's vascular (blood vessel) system, is one of the leading causes of health problems and death in the world's developed countries. Avoid eating too many fatty foods, get regular exercise, and do not smoke. It's never too early to follow a healthy lifestyle!

Heart *A Close-Up of the Heart*

The heart and how its "feelings" influence our daily lives is a favorite subject of singers, poets, and playwrights. Love, courage, and kindness come from the brain, not from the heart—yet even the clever brain relies on the heart to survive.

Pear Shaped

The typical heart shape often used to represent feelings of love is inaccurate. Your heart is shaped more like a squashed pear lying on its side. The heart is a muscular, hollow bag with four chambers. Its two upper chambers, called atria, are smaller and have thinner walls than the two lower chambers, called ventricles. Each atrium connects to the ventricle below it by a flaplike valve. Blood enters the heart via the atria and gets pumped out of the heart via the ventricles.

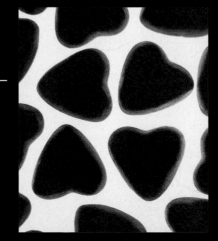

Everyone recognizes the typical cartoon heart shape, but it is inaccurate. A human heart looks more like a squashed pear or a potato with a pointy end.

Pump, pump, pump. Your heart never stops. Mechanical pumps might last 10 or 20 years, but the amazing heart muscle beats for many, many decades.

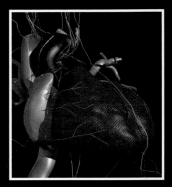

Two in One

The heart is not a single pump, but two pumps side by side. The right pump has an upper atrium and a lower ventricle. Oxygen-poor blood from all around the body enters the right atrium and passes through the tricuspid valve into the right ventricle. From there, it flows to the lungs. Oxygen-rich blood returning from the lungs enters the left atrium, goes through the mitral valve to the left ventricle, and then flows through the body. So the body has two circulations—the short, pulmonary circulation between the heart and lungs and the long, systemic circulation from the heart to the rest of the body.

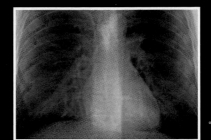

Medical technology allows doctors to "see" your heart without cutting you open. This colored chest X ray shows the heart in pink. Another procedure, a coronary angiogram, outlines the heart's blood vessels, while an echocardiogram displays the beating heart's motion in "real time."

The special muscle of the heart, called cardiac muscle, or myocardium, never stops working. The heart needs a continuing blood supply.

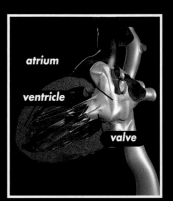

atrium

ventricle

valve

The heart's smaller upper chambers are the right atrium and left atrium. Each pumps blood through a special valve to its connecting lower right or left chamber, or ventricle. The ventricles push the blood out into the blood vessels.

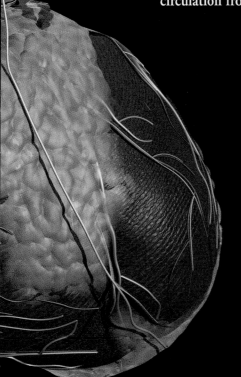

🖐 TRY IT YOURSELF

Lie on your back and raise your head a little. Try to see signs of your heart's steady beating. Now look at your abdomen. It moves up and down as you breathe in and out. Watch closely. You should also see a slight fluttering caused by your heartbeat.

Most animals have some sort of pumping organ that helps circulate their body fluids. Usually animals only need one pump, but an earthworm has five "hearts" in a row along its main blood vessel.

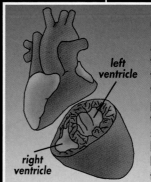

🫀 CHAMBERS

A cross section shows the difference between the two ventricles. The thinner right ventricle pumps blood just to the lungs. The much stronger and thicker left ventricle pumps blood to the rest of the body.

left ventricle

right ventricle

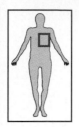

Your heart beats almost every second, most of the time without you noticing it. When you are relaxed, your heartbeat is slow and steady. When you exercise, your heart beats faster and harder, and you may feel it pounding inside your chest.

Blood Enters the Heart

The heart beats with a smooth, continuous motion, sending the blood on its one-way journey though the body. Blood always enters the heart via the upper chambers. Each thin-walled atrium only needs to pump its blood down to the connecting lower chamber on its side of the heart. As the atria contract, they squeeze blood through a funnel-shaped valve into the adjoining ventricle.

Our hearts respond to fright by pumping faster and harder. The brain triggers the release of the hormone (message-carrying chemical) adrenaline into the blood to cause a rapid, instantaneous "fight or flight" reaction.

Tiny electrical signals passing through the myocardium cause the heartbeat. Chest sensors can detect and record these signals as spiky lines (right) called an electrocardiogram (EKG or ECG).

IN FOCUS
Heart Valves

The funnel-shaped heart valves between atria and ventricles consist of a tough, leathery material held open by cords. The right valve is the tricuspid. The left valve is the bicuspid, or mitral.

Blood Leaves the Heart

Next the thicker ventricle muscle walls contract, squeezing the blood within them much harder. The valves between the ventricles and atriums snap shut to prevent backflow. Blood flows out from the right ventricle to the lungs through the pulmonary valve or from the left ventricle through the aortic valve to the rest of the body.

HEART BEATS

After the atria fill (1), they pump (contract), pushing blood through the open valves (2) to the ventricles. When the ventricles pump, the valves shut to prevent backflow (3). The valves open again as the ventricles contract, and blood rushes out into the arteries (4). The valves snapping closed make the familiar "lubb-dup" heartbeat sound.

Smaller animals have faster heart rates than humans. A tiny shrew's heart, which is smaller than a peanut, beats up to 1,000 times a minute. Only rarely does the human heart rate reach even 200 beats a minute.

Blood makes up about one-twelfth of the weight of the body.

A woman has about four to five quarts of blood, and a man has about five to six quarts of blood.

Only about one-twentieth of the body's blood is in the capillaries at a time. About three-quarters of the blood is in the veins.

Thrombosis is the presence of a thrombus, or blood clot, in a blood vessel or the heart.

Blood *Liquid for Life*

Our red, thick, sticky, sweet, sealing, healing blood is truly a river of life. It carries hundreds of dissolved chemicals, sugars, minerals, and salts that perform vital jobs every second of our lives.

Why Red?

Bright red blood contains plenty of oxygen. The oxygen attaches to hemoglobin, a chemical carried by one of blood's main components, the red blood cells (RBCs). A drop of blood as big as this letter "o" contains 25 million RBCs. When they absorb oxygen in the lungs, the blood turns bright red. As the oxygen-rich blood travels around the body, the oxygen passes from the RBCs into the surrounding tissues. This transfer occurs in the capillaries, the tiniest of blood vessels. In the exchange, the blood's color changes from bright red to darker reddish purple.

Full of Goodness

White blood cells (WBCs) are another main type of cell carried by the blood. White blood cells clean the blood and fight diseases. Parts of cells called platelets also float along in the blood. At a cut or injury, platelets clump together to form a thick, sticky lump called a clot. The clot seals the cut and stops bleeding. Blood also carries energy in the form of glucose—"blood sugar"—for use by muscles.

HEALTH WATCH

Do you know your blood group? There are two main sets of groups—A, B, or O, and rhesus positive and negative. These groups indicate how the blood will react if mixed with blood from another person. If someone needs replacement blood (a transfusion), the groups must match. If not matched, the added blood will clot, clog vessels, and cause serious medical problems—and sometimes even death.

Blood banks, hospitals, and medical centers collect and use thousands of units of blood every day. People who are ill, injured, or having surgery may die without a blood transfusion. Blood donations help save lives.

Hydroponic crops are grown without soil. The water around their roots contains all the nutrients and minerals they need. Your blood is like that water—it carries all the substances your body needs.

IN FOCUS
Wound Healing

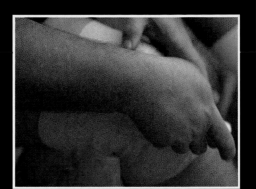

Some injuries are too large or too deep for a blood clot to seal on its own. Emergency first aid, such as applying pressure and a bandage, will slow blood loss and keep the wound clean and free of germs.

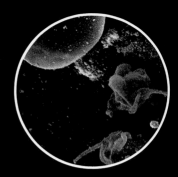

Within seconds of an injury, sticky microthreads of fibrin form in the blood. Red blood cells and platelets get tangled in the fibrin, and the platelets produce even more sticky substances and threads. Eventually, a blood clot forms to plug the gap.

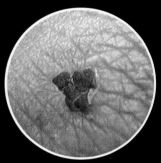

After a few days, the clot hardens into a scab to protect the area while the damaged tissue repairs itself.

TRY IT YOURSELF

Whirl one arm around like a windmill several times. Quickly hold both hands together and compare their colors. The force of whirling causes your blood to flow down into your hand but not back up. Your whirled hand should look much redder than the other one.

BLOOD CONTENT

Blood for testing is often separated into different layers. More than half of blood is yellowish, watery plasma that carries nutrients. White blood cells fight infection and disease. Red blood cells carry oxygen.

The aorta, the body's main artery, is about 0.9 inches wide. Blood surges through it at 0.6 miles per hour.

A typical smaller artery is 0.2 inches wide. Blood flows along at 0.1 miles per hour.

A capillary is just 0.03–0.06 inches long and only 0.0003 inches wide. Blood, oxygen, and nutrients seep in and out of its walls.

A large vein is 1.2 inches wide, but its blood moves slowly, with almost no pressure.

HEALTH WATCH

Arteries and veins that serve the heart muscle itself are called coronary vessels. If a coronary artery hardens and clogs, it blocks the blood and oxygen supply to the heart muscle. Partial blockages may lead to angina, which causes chest pain, breathlessness, and sweating. Complete coronary blockage can cause a heart attack.

Blood *Blood Vessels*

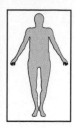

Blood does not slosh around the body like water in a barrel. It flows through a network of blood vessels—arteries, capillaries, and veins—that differ in size, structure, and function.

Wave of Pressure

Arteries carry blood away from the heart. The largest arteries are about as big around as your thumb. Arteries have thick walls that are tough and stretchy to withstand the pressure of blood as it surges out of the heart. Artery walls throughout the body bulge with each heartbeat.

Too Small to See

Arteries branch as they leave the heart, becoming narrower and thinner-walled arterioles. They lead to all body areas, including the heart itself. Finally, they divide into the smallest vessels of all—capillaries. Some capillaries function as arteries, others as veins. Capillary walls are one cell thick, so that substances such as oxygen and nutrients can seep out into tissues and waste products can seep in for disposal by the blood.

Wide and Floppy

Veins return blood to the heart. Blood loses most of its pressure by the time it travels through the arteries into the capillaries. Capillaries join to make wider vessels with thin and floppy walls. Blood flows through veins much more slowly than through arteries.

It takes high air pressure to blow up a balloon. Each heartbeat causes a surge of blood pressure and creates balloonlike bulges that travel along the walls of your arteries.

Tunnels allow passage of people, supplies, and utility cables around an obstruction, such as a mountain or a river. Blood vessels function as miniature tunnels that carry blood and its life-giving cargo to all areas of the body.

IN FOCUS
Blood Vessels

Capillaries (right) are so narrow that even the smallest cells in the body, the red blood cells, must pass through them in single file.

The maze of pipes, tubes, ducts, vessels, and channels of a chemical factory or oil refinery is nothing compared to the body's network of blood vessels. If your body were the same size as one of those plants, its vessels would need a building 31 miles long.

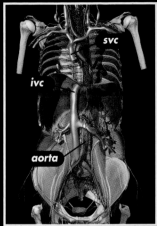

The aorta's branches lead to the head, arms, abdomen, and legs. The main veins returning to the heart from the upper body are the superior vena cava (svc) and from the lower body, the inferior vena cava (ivc).

TRY IT YOURSELF

Look at blood vessels on yourself or an older family member. The veins just under the skin on the back of the hand, inside of the wrist, or forearm are easy to see. Notice how the veins join as they go back up the arm to the heart.

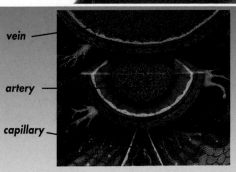

vein

artery

capillary

VESSELS UP CLOSE

An artery's wall is mostly muscle. The brain automatically controls the width of arteries by contracting arterial muscles to make them narrower and reduce blood flow or relaxing the muscles to widen the vessels and increase blood flow. A capillary is five times thinner than a human hair and shorter than this "i." A venous capillary joins to a venule, which joins to a vein. A vein is wide and flexible, with very thin walls. Flaplike valves in the main veins prevent backflow.

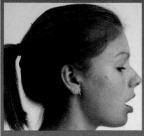

Blood *Fighting Diseases*

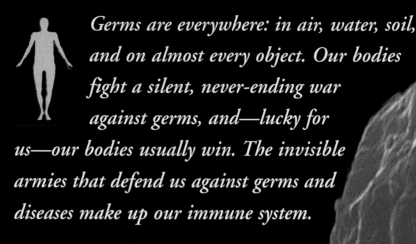

Germs are everywhere: in air, water, soil, and on almost every object. Our bodies fight a silent, never-ending war against germs, and—lucky for us—our bodies usually win. The invisible armies that defend us against germs and diseases make up our immune system.

White Blood Cells to the Rescue

An "army" of thousands of white blood cells in every drop of blood includes some of the best "soldiers" in the immune system. Some types of WBCs attack germs directly, "eating" them whole. Others produce antibodies that stick onto germs so that they die. Still others keep the blood clean by absorbing tiny pieces of floating waste. White cells can move out of the blood and into other body parts, especially into the mysterious clear fluid called lymph.

Like border guards who check the passports of people entering a country, the body's immune system is constantly on the lookout for germs that can harm the body.

A vaccination injects germs that have been made harmless into the body. This gives the immune system a "blueprint" for developing resistance to that disease.

The "Other" Circulation

Like blood, lymph is a liquid that flows around the body, but in the lymph vessels, a "tube" system separate from the circulatory system. Lymph forms around and between body cells, tissues, and organs. It collects in small tubes that join to form larger lymph vessels. In some areas, the vessels widen to form lumps called lymph nodes. The lymph nodes are packed with white blood cells and other disease-fighting cells. If germs invade, the lymph nodes enlarge as the WBCs multiply and attack the germs. We call these enlarged lymph nodes "swollen glands."

Lymph vessels collect lymph fluid from all around the body. The main lymph vessels connect to the circulatory system near the heart, where the lymph seeps into the bloodstream.

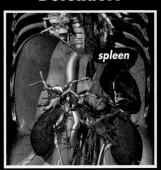
spleen

Your spleen stores blood, recycles old RBCs, and makes new white blood cells.

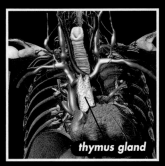
thymus gland

The pale thymus gland helps "train" white blood cells to recognize germs. It shrinks greatly after childhood.

TRY IT YOURSELF

Have you ever had a sideache—a sharp pain, usually on your upper left side—while running or exercising? This pain may be caused when the spleen contracts (tightens) to pour its stores of blood into the bloodstream. The extra blood helps carry more oxygen to the muscles and relieves the pain.

VESSELS AND NODES

Lymph fluid flows much more slowly than blood. With no pump to push it along, the pressure of normal body movements squeezes lymph through the lymphatic vessels. Valves in the main vessels assure a one-way flow of the lymph. Compartments inside a typical lymph node (right) contain lymph fluid and many kinds of white blood cells to help fight diseases and infections.

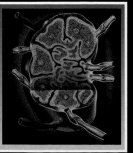

Glossary

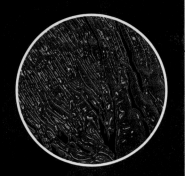

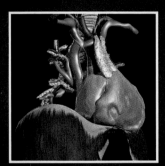

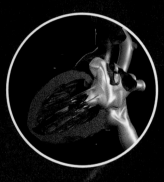

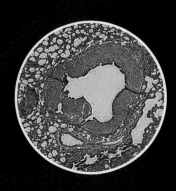

abdomen the lower main body, from the base of the chest down to the hips. It contains many of the organs of digestion and waste disposal.

allergy the body's defensive reaction to harmful germs. An allergy can also develop against harmless substances such as plant pollens or house dust.

alveoli microscopic, bubble-shaped air sacs in the lungs where oxygen passes from air into the blood.

arteriole a blood vessel that carries blood away from the heart. It is thinner than an artery but larger than a capillary.

artery a strong, thick-walled blood vessel that carries blood away from the heart.

atrium one of the two upper chambers of the heart. The atria receive blood flowing in from the veins and pass it to their respective ventricles below.

bronchi the larger airways in the chest that branch from the base of the trachea.

bronchiole an air tube narrower than bronchi but thicker than the tiniest, terminal bronchioles.

capillary the narrowest, microscopic blood vessels with walls one cell thick to allow the exchange of gases and blood products to tissues and organs.

carbon dioxide a gaseous waste product made by the body as it releases the energy from food. Blood carries it to the lungs, where it is breathed out.

cartilage a strong, smooth, shiny, slightly flexible substance that forms the nose, ears, and larynx and covers the ends of bones in a joint.

cells tiny building blocks of the body, which in their billions make up larger organs, such as bones, muscles, and skin.

cilia tiny hairlike projections of microscopic cells found in many body areas. Cilia lining the airways wave, or "beat," to keep the sticky, germ-gathering mucus moving up and out of the lungs.

diaphragm a large, dome-shaped sheet of muscle at the base of the thorax. It is the main muscle for breathing.

fibrin thin strings of protein that help form a blood clot.

involuntary muscle muscle that we cannot control at will, such as that found in the airways; also called unstriated or visceral muscle.

larynx voicebox.

muscle soft tissues that contract to move body parts.

nasal chambers the air spaces inside the nose through which air passes as we breathe in and out.

oxygen a colorless, tasteless, odorless gas that makes up one-fifth of air. Oxygen helps the body release energy from food.

pharynx the throat area that leads from the nose and mouth into the esophagus. (A sore throat is called pharyngitis.)

platelets very tiny disks that float in plasma and help form blood clots to stop bleeding.

pleurae smooth, slippery, baglike layers that wrap around the lungs and allow them to change size with each breath.

red blood cells (RBCs) the tiniest cells in blood. They contain hemoglobin to carry oxygen.

respiration 1: for the entire body, breathing air in and out to obtain oxygen and get rid of carbon dioxide 2: in a cell, the chemical breakdown of blood sugar (glucose) using oxygen to release energy in a process called cellular respiration.

sinuses honeycomblike air spaces within the skull around the face that connect to the main nasal airway via ducts.

terminal bronchioles the thinnest air tubes in the lungs that end at groups of microscopic air sacs called alveoli.

thorax the chest region from the neck and shoulders down to the abdomen. It contains the heart and main blood vessels, the lungs, and the main airways.

trachea the windpipe. It extends from the base of the larynx down to the site where it branches into two smaller airways, the bronchi.

ventricle one of the two large lower chambers of the heart. It receives blood flowing from the atrium above and pumps it out into the arteries to the lungs or the entire body.

venule a blood vessel that carries blood from organs and tissues toward the heart. It is wider than a capillary but not as large as a vein.

vocal folds small flaps or ridges in the larynx that vibrate (shake very fast) to produce the sounds of the voice.

white blood cells (WBCs) whitish blood cells that help the body fight illnesses, diseases, and infections.

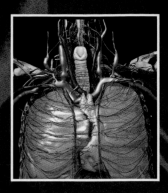

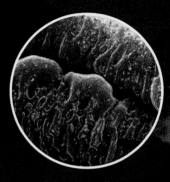

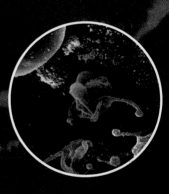

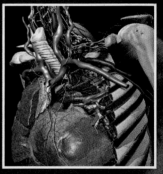

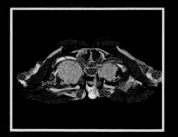

METRIC CONVERSION TABLE

LENGTH/DISTANCE

1 inch = 2.54 centimeters
1 foot = 12 inches = 30 centimeters
1 mile = 1.6 kilometers

SPEED

1 mile per hour (mph) =
      1.6 kilometers per hour (kph)
25 mph = 40 kph

WEIGHT

1 ounce = 28 grams
16 ounces = 1 pound
      = 0.45 kilogram

VOLUME

1 pint = 0.47 liter
1 quart = 0.95 liter
1 gallon = 3.8 liters

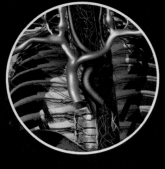
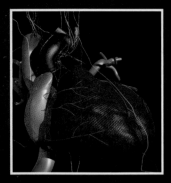
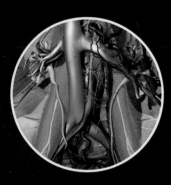
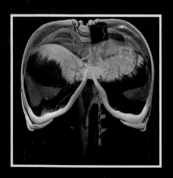
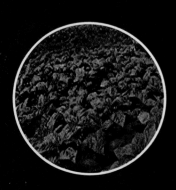

I n d e x